FINISHING LINE PRESS
www.finishinglinepress.com

AF472064

Sorrow and Hope

poems by

Paul Lobo Portugés

Finishing Line Press
Georgetown, Kentucky

Sorrow and Hope

ISBN 978-1-944899-06-6 First Edition

ACKNOWLEDGMENTS

Some of these poems appeared in: *the bluest eye, ifandwhen, Rosebud, A. Bradstreet, Negative Suck, SLO Festival Anthology, Literature Today, Poetry Pacific, Naugatuck River Review, Overthrowing Capitalism: An Anthology, Floricanto, Truthdig, Knot Magazine, La Bloga, Sore Dove Press: Pocket Nugget #5, Paris Lit, The Border Crossed Us Anthology, Spectrum: L.A. Anthology,* and other magazines I can't remember.

Editor: Christen Kincaid

Cover Art: Paul Portugés

Author Photo: Bill Barrett

Cover Design: Elizabeth Maines

Printed in the USA on acid-free paper.
Order online: www.finishinglinepress.com
also available on amazon.com

Author inquiries and mail orders:
Finishing Line Press
P. O. Box 1626
Georgetown, Kentucky 40324
U. S. A.

Table of Contents

for my family and friends

El Norte

—for the children of El Salvador, Guatemala, and Honduras

When he was 8 in the white heat of El Infiernito
Guarding their fruit truck they murdered his father
And the squawking blue birds of his young hope
Flew away into the gut of lovely night
And the proud red plums he held rolled down
The blood alley as rain fell like broken feathers

When he was in the flesh of his blue youth
Songs turned to skeletons in his best friend's eyes
They smiled as they slit her white naked throat
And stuffed panties in her red mouth of dreams
That dia de los muertos she became the flowers of graves
Seeing a body was nothing anymore

When he was 12, narcos beat him blind
So he couldn't see their skulls of black death
His tearless baby cousins could only look on
Santa Muerte made him lick the white thighs of crack
"You'll feel freed like a bird entering
A red cloud in the bruise of blue night"

His dirty government can't pull up its pants.
"If your house is burning, jump out the window"
So he took the lazy train of hopeful skeletons
With a handful of plums and his invisible hope
And crossed the red white and blue border of eagles
Like a beautiful feather on the veins of lonely wind

Sorrow and Hope #1

I shall never be friendly with roses after the righteous darkness
Under moonless dirt sans blue air or whatever holier follows
Nor listen to my river boys fingering moonlight on their daisy girls' arms
Riding their loins blind to time in their skeleton skin
Denying the future after dead earth as they happy like bees flee
Thinking their children will carry on with holiday flowers
Believing DNA fables imagined one morning drunk with Eden's light
Nor shall they nor I dance in a heavenly re-birth breath after breath

But my bent over shadow and thou shall now under the hangman's sun
Feed on love's joy and not wait for the cock of tomorrow
But we'll crow slap happy for the jubilee song in trees
Taking note of the mortal stories in falling leaves that burn in time's war
And like fools for laughter ponder the everlasting in my love's prayers
That lights up my earthbound poems and gives hope at the end of days

Sorrow and Hope #2

When the words of our song are buried in the bones of our mouth
And children are the poem's voice fading in space and time
Before or after the planet's oblivion when even guns are no matter
And we're blue because the acid of rape and the capitalism of war
And even God's stars are a black hole above this hell below
And we've lost our invitation to salvation knowing we're nothing
Not even a nano in a molecule of El Jahweh's wrathful shadow
Nor even a burning memory in the genetic maw that was our body

Then in a murmuration of starlings or an anthem's musical flag
Or a child's happy steps in the mud or the scent of a lover's desire
Or even a best mate barking when we come home drunk
Somehow we because our soul spits at death's horsemen
And we're reading this still breathing with a kick in our smile
We don't give a damn because the sun's out and there's hope there's time

Sorrow and Hope #3

I watch crows watching me garden in the low workaday sun
As lavender bees chase holiday girls shouting their truant freedom
Past our shore laughing cottage where finches sing the day asleep
And my sometime love weaves a satisfied memoir of longing
Before her altar of computers that feeds on lonely night
And my leftover sister re-lives our father's angry passing
While I'm all about our dirty planet as though it matters knowing
Soon patriarchy and vanity will be dust after the sixth extinction

Yet I still admire joyous clouds telling stories imagined or not
Because crows bees wife family dirt the dying sun
Are forever heaven's book of never now we want to believe
And the ring of our tangled vows and nights of shooting stars
Give us hope as we share warm bread and garden flowers
Before we are unread names in weathered stone and are gone utterly gone

Sorrow and Hope #4

The sorrow that hides in breathing is God's virus
We're born to die have children and even sunrise
But nothing halts death that guardian angel
Hovering even when we are sweet as lips and surely
When a child coughs or you lose your old way in a familiar place
Or when silent night feeds on thee and festers
In our lonely neighbors because we have what they want
Or in just wars of child carnage that turns murderers into heroes

But as it is so we can put the infinite darkness to sleep
And embrace the god given sky gladly learning to be like waves
Shoaling cresting gracefully back to the ever same ocean
Like you and me and your children and their children's children
As we rise drunk with love singing war no more though sleeping with grief
And finally alone as at birth fade into everlasting sorrow and hope

Sorrow and Hope #5

Jihadists bonsai the soul's enemy with a testament of hate
While U.S. gamers release drones that make mothers cry
And Jefferson's 3/5 black boys kneel in their blood with hands up
And roofied sisters are taken by boozed fraternities of brothers

The trafficked poor sweat in hip houses of the cosmopolitan
The richey rich shoot up with barrels of dinosaur bones
And the leftover old get stacked up in houses of morphine
And half the sky curses the violence of their husbands and lovers

Kids deny tomorrow while smoking the sky until it's methane
With plastic and hamburgers they hate mother gaia
And don't remember the human universe before they were wired
And in porn's skin they lick faceless pixels while texting simulated breath

Immigrants of the past worshiped sun and blood of their kin
So no wonder today's children worship a virtual god of sin

The Comfort Woman of Korea

The day she was sent
with other girls to become
a comfort woman
she wept as they watched
peach blossoms in the wind

At night soldiers came
to her until early morning
20 or so…a Captain broke
the bones of her soul
she didn't care if she died

They rounded up younger girls
after they tore their genitals
she could hear them
crying as the wet earth
covered them with night

She's learned to accept
the suffering though still
hopes for justice because
she dies again & again
when the peach blossoms fall

East Los

Cigarette butts make unusual mosaics of cancer
in the so-called lawn of the heavily policed
park on Mr. Whittier's boulevard
while gringo kings brag about breeder reactors
and beget ribbons of fear as they hunt pussy
in los vatos of the City of Angels
near a footloose muchacho throwing his paper plane
past billboards of powdered white pudenda
admired by hairless blonde never-never-land boys
wrestling in surviving dandelions
as lowriders drag their jails of anger burning
rubber past lonely Joe's t.v. repair shop
where booty commercials flash upside down
in the smog streaked neon window of America's hunger
for objects of sex shattered by bullets
that curse barrio poets who eat them
like dulces then spit out histories of pain

Flies

(after Li Bai)

flies swarm
a half-eaten raven

dew lingers
on the wild grasses

on the banks
of dry Los Osos creek

nothing but leaf skeletons
not even morning bird calls

broken eucalyptus lean
toward the blue

a cold wind waves
through the brown hills

I wait barely breathing
where are you

The Poetry of Air

It was her wetness he wanted
chasing her in the fog of love
to lose his sorrow beneath her skirt

He whispered "Sorry, I'm not dead yet"
after she wouldn't cum
knowing the future is lonely

(It was just a matter of time
when she's younger under the knife
because love is not enough)

Listening to her moaning
while she slept he knew
she would sadly betray him

After their sons leave them
before his name is last spoken
and he is the poetry of air

he's an unfortunate…

he's an unfortunate
citizen of the corporate needle

a dumpster friend
of alley leftovers

ignored daily
by macho headlines

of little dick wars

Against the Living Air

Our friendly brother's body ashes
scatter in a zodiac of celestial wind
blowing off kind Pacifico
across the forgiving earth he planted
each dead spring into every summer and fall

Under the safe hip California sky
our only God fearing friend (in my crying brain)
romanced freed thoughts of intellectual tears
those rare bourgeoisie nights of breathless
friendly felt talk about the warming air's future

That Southern drawl and cautious laugh
gone now only his ashes falling about us
we pray he's eternally safe remembering
his love for the blue Santa Barbara manzanita
the geese honking sky of his homophobic green Virginia

We all can still hear the dried veins
of his brutal voice saved in our memories
(he asked me to lay pennies on his lids)
our gone good friend gone for good
safe with his Chagall's bearded Creator
who birthed us all promising we'll see Him soon

but for fortune…

but
for
fortune
homeless
rise

in
the
moist
sunrise
&
hunt

for
a
place
to
shit

FGM

"A real woman never cries. I will remove this dirt,
and you will become clean, a real Muslim."

The women sang and danced
In the morning mist by the river
The wind played in the trees
As they tied her to a bramble bush
To numb her forever down there
And the drums beat louder and louder

The songs and wind in the trees stopped:
"Please Grandmother, don't, please!"
The razor was wet with the blood of other girls
"In the name of Allah Most Gracious, Most Merciful"
Then she felt the terrible pain between her legs
And the drums beat louder and louder

They covered her mouth and cut out the dirt
Slicing into the heart of her skull
Then shut her inside to bleed and cry
Her Grandmother brought water and food
While friends prayed and danced for her joy
And the drums beat louder and louder

Her Father told her "What's done is done"
As he blessed her and shook her hand
Her Mother wept and sang a song of love
Gave her chocolates & oranges and lit a fire
So she would not go barren if she healed
And the drums beat louder and louder

When she finally returned to her family
A village ceremony celebrated her passage
Glad she was now ready to be with men
Though barely eleven, finally a woman, pure
She hates the wind in the trees the singing of the river
Where the drums beat louder and louder

Ikkyu

Ikkyu grew rooted in the banyan tree
until flowering then invented consciousness
of twilight until he surrendered to mountains
of babble and joyously entered the beckoning grave
with compassionate tears and a belly of laughter

Ikkyu copied his Bodhisattva poems
from the breath of children the water of waters
our Zen future after cities chronicled poverty's lips
preparing us for stones of sorrow for human dust
all the while studying light the dew drops on a lotus blossom

Ikkyu blazed crazy wisdom paths
through seasons of everyday hell
becoming now my handsome sound
and recurring dream of him handing me
the glass laurel of his mouth

Ikkyu the Buddha not Buddhist not getting caught up
year after year in the brush of the brush
tucking his poems asleep until they stir inside like morning
Ikkyu the dancer of dance patiently watching each
breath each wonderful rise and fall

begging for work...

begging
for
work
or
change

she
screams
at
the
silent
sky

about
children
she
aborted

by corporate t.v.…

by		
corporate	hookup	
t.v.	skin	&
light	deep	manufactured
media	with	want
teens	commercial	
	sex	

bedside guns…

bedside guns
chemical air

tough living
in God bless America

risky if you're black
brown Amerindian

or see with the eyes of Asia
or even a white woman

in the heat
of violent night

dicey even
to make love

globalized males…

globalized		
males	passing	
undress	by	youth
hip	sexualized	bigger
women	by	&
	pretty	video

she was afraid…

she
was
afraid
the
swallows

wouldn't
come
this
spring

what
with
the
war
and
all

An Angry Kiss

Rickshaw diesel air rises
above a junk field as I pass
down the fly ruled streets
hoping for an apple

A flower vendor sings
to the swarming bees
in the sticky Asian afternoon

Everyone is calm

A young bodhisattva smokes
a quiet cigarette in the rusted
backseat of his waiting bus

Scrounging for food
behind a foreign restaurant
barefoot a small bronze woman
holds tight her baby
pulling at the silk scarf woven
in her silk black hair

With a terrible grin
she calls me "Joe"
and blows an angry kiss
off the tip of her bruised hand

High above bi-colored
eight-sided happy kites
are mastered by tireless children
running along the left thigh
of the sleeping golden Buddha

Black Lung

He gets the darkness
Playing with my son
He'll say, "Well, buddy
I got to put you down."
His son'll say, "Run papa run."

He faces his Mt. Everest every day.
Sometimes he makes it to the top,
Sometimes he just don't.
It's like he's got a heavy sack
On each black lung.

Some days friends visit.
He can hear them whispering
"He's done" and supposes he might be.
It's sure as shit
He's not getting no better.

At night he thinks to himself
He's a waste of time.
He watches the lantern
On the porch hoping
It don't go out.

He loved workin' underground.
Hell, he still dreams about it.
It can't be this bad—
And then he realizes
"You ain't seen nothing yet."

Gaza

" Forget the philosophy of bullets, we are tired of funerals."
M. Darwish

He closes the door to darkness and bends like an old tree over his son
Wraps himself around him with the calm of a summer shade
While terror bombs scatter butterflies in the happy flowers
And shatter the faint smile on the boy's quivering lips

They wait with pain for all the dying children to stop crying
If only a thousand prayers would lift them to heaven
Where the stars are the happy faces of kids skipping in the clouds.
He never found them under his father's father's house of stone now dust

And when he wept for his true love she had already become a galaxy
As he lifted her from the rubble her heart became the song of birds
He hears every morning when they visit her grave of roses and tears
Under the tree he and she climbed as children imagining happy stories in
clouds

after hot weeks…

after hot weeks
picking shoveling

sleeping in junkyard cars
nos hermanos cross

the imaginary border
to their tossed away lives

when a child dies…

<table>
<tr><td>when
a
child
dies</td><td>
it's
something
you
keep</td><td>

in
you
like
a
bomb</td></tr>
</table>

Paul Lobo Portugés—reared in Merkel, West Texas, until saved by UCLA, the American Film Institute, and UC Berkeley. Taught creative writing at UCSB, UC Berkeley, USC, SBCC, Cuesta College, and the University of Provence. Proud father of two sons. Books include *The Visionary Poetics of Allen Ginsberg, Saving Grace, Hands Across the Earth, The Flower Vendor, Paper Song, Aztec Birth, The Body Electric Journal, The Silent Spring of Rachel Carson, Jack and Marilyn* (Plainview Press, 2016), *Ginsberg: On Tibetan Buddhism, Mantras, and Drugs, Breaking Bread, Mao—1,000 Poems for Revolution* (forthcoming). Poems are scattered in small magazines (*Hambone, Chelsea, River Styx) and anthologies (Overthrowing Capitalism, The Asian Writer, Naropa Anthology, Spectrum—So Cal Poets Anthology*), across the Americas, Europe, Latin America, and Asia. Wrote a few films including *The Look of Love, Behind the Veil, Shakespeare's Last Bed, Fire From the Mountain. Poetry videos include To My Beloved, Kiss, The Lonely Wind, Lovers, Of Her I Sing, Fathermine, Stones from Heaven, The Killing Fields of Darfur, Who on Earth.* Received awards from the National Endowment, the Ford Foundation, the Fulbright Commission, *et al.*

www.ingramcontent.com/pod-product-compliance
Ingram Content Group UK Ltd.
Pitfield, Milton Keynes, MK11 3LW, UK
UKHW042011190726
13854UKWH00005B/2239

9 781944 899066